1 MONTH OF
FREE
READING

at

www.ForgottenBooks.com

By purchasing this book you are
eligible for one month membership to
ForgottenBooks.com, giving you
unlimited access to our entire
collection of over 1,000,000 titles via
our web site and mobile apps.

To claim your free month visit:
www.forgottenbooks.com/free184389

ISBN 978-0-484-90218-2
PIBN 10184389

Forgotten Books is a registered trademark of FB &c Ltd.
Copyright © 2018 FB &c Ltd.
FB &c Ltd, Dalton House, 60 Windsor Avenue, London, SW19 2RR.
Company number 08720141. Registered in England and Wales.

For support please visit www.forgottenbooks.com

REPORT

OF THE

George William Curtis Memorial Committee

WITH

MEMORIAL ADDRESS

OF

Hon. Carl Schurz

ORANGE, NEW JERSEY:
THE CHRONICLE PRESS
1905

PROEM.

The National Civil Service Reform League met in Baltimore in April 1902. As usual, George William Curtis occupied his post as President, and as usual the meeting closed with a dinner given by the local Association, which was attended by a large number of guests, ladies and gentlemen. When Mr. Curtis rose to speak he was received with a burst of enthusiasm which has seldom been equaled. Again and again he essayed to speak, and again and again the applause broke out anew. It was an expression alike of admiration for the leader and intense affection for the friend. Tears came to the eyes of those most unaccustomed to outward exhibition of their feelings, and those in the company with one accord rose to their feet with prolonged cheers.

When at last quiet reigned we listened to a speech such as only Mr. Curtis could utter. It was always his custom to prepare himself with care for even such an occasion as this, and I have before me as I write his original notes for this address. I have been repeatedly asked to publish them, but the speech as delivered so far transcended that which he had outlined that I have felt that all who heard it would prefer to retain the impression of that which they heard, rather than read that which he expected to say. I will only quote his closing words:

"It is the spring of the year, and it is the springtime of reform. It is not the harvest, but it is the sowing. The blossoms which open in this soft spring air, are flowers only, not yet fruit. But they are promises of the summer, and the fruit is sure. They are voluntary pledges of nature, and in its benign administration in which seed time and harvest never fail, those pledges will be completely fulfilled. The little twig of Magna Charta has become the wide-spreading tree of English liberty. Our bud of reform will become a system of honester politics."

As, after midnight, we drove through the bright moonlight to the home of our host, he seemed palpitating with the warmth of his reception, and quoting from Tom Moore—was it not?

> "The best of all ways
> To lengthen our days,
> Is to steal a few hours from the night,
> My dear,"——

he came to my room after our arrival, and there remained long, loath to commit himself to the arms of sleep.

The fiat had gone forth and he knew it not. Occasionally he came to the city after his return to his home, but soon these trips must be given up, and by the beginning of July he was confined to his room, suffering intensely. Possibly the last of those not of his home family, I saw him on the twenty-first of July. We could speak but little. He knew that the end was at hand, and he felt that there was so much to be done! As we clasped hands for the last time he said only, "Give my love to all my friends,"—and I here transmit the message.

On the thirty-first of August he died, and on the second of September, under a kind autumn sun, we laid away what was left of the noble form, on the hillside fronting the bay, in the Moravian Cemetery on Staten Island.

WILLIAM POTTS.

Report of Committee.

On the eighteenth of November, 1893, a number of gentlemen nominated as a Memorial Committee at several previous informal gatherings, met at dinner at the University Club, as the guests of Joseph W. Harper, and organized by the selection of Seth Low as Chairman, William Potts as Secretary, and William L. Trenholm as Treasurer.

The note of appointment of the committee is as follows:

IN MEMORY OF GEORGE WILLIAM CURTIS.

We, the undersigned, earnestly feeling that it is due to those that are to follow us that we should publicly testify to the unvarying courtesy, the genius for friendship, the literary accomplishment, the oratorical power, the high ideal of citizenship, the devotion to duty, the purity of life, and the nobility of character of the late George William Curtis by some appropriate memorial, have thought well to designate the following gentlemen as members of a Committee charged with the duty of determining the character of such memorial, with receiving the needed subscriptions therefor, and with full power to establish the same, *viz.*:

HENRY M. ALDEN
EDWARD CARY
JOHN W. CHADWICK
JOSEPH H. CHOATE
ROBERT COLLYER
RICHARD WATSON GILDER
PARKE GODWIN
J. HENRY HARPER
JOSEPH W. HARPER
EASTMAN JOHNSON
SETH LOW
A. R. MACDONOUGH

OSWALD OTTENDORFER
JOHN E. PARSONS
HORACE PORTER
HENRY C. POTTER
WILLIAM POTTS
THEODORE ROOSEVELT
CARL SCHURZ
WM. H. THOMSON
WM. L. TRENHOLM
CORNELIUS VANDERBILT
WM. R. WARE
CHAS. DUDLEY WARNER

Feeling entire confidence in the judgment of this Committee, we place the matter in their hands without restriction.

Lyman Abbot.
Charles F. Adams.
C. K. Adams.
Joseph Adams.
Felix Adler.
A. Agassiz.
Wm. A. Aiken.
Henry M. Alden.
Chas. Chaflin Allen.
James Lane Allen.
Reese F. Alsop.
Chas. G. Ames.
John F. Andrew.
E. Benj. Andrews.
James B. Angell.
D. F. Appleton.
William W. Appleton.
Sam P. Avery.
Sam'l D. Babcock.
Truman J. Backus.
Danford N. Barney.
Amelia E. Barr.
Samuel J. Barrows.
Arlo Bates.
T. F. Bayard.
Charles C. Beaman.
Carroll Beckwith.
Joel Benton.
Charles E. Bessey.
Albert Bierstadt.
William Henry Bishop.
William Bispham.
Charles J. Bonaparte.
G. T. Bonner.
V. Botta.
R. R. Bowker.
Samuel Bowles.
Hjalmar H. Boyesen.
Martin Brimmer.
Arthur Brooks.
J. G. Brown.
Junius Henri Browne.

Clarence Clough Buel.
Sara C. Bull.
H. C. Bunner.
Frances Hodgson Burnett.
John Burroughs.
Silas W. Burt.
Howard Russell Butler.
Nicholas Murray Butler.
William Allen Butler.
Geo. W. Cable.
John L. Cadwalader.
Will Carleton.
Franklin Carter.
Edward Cary.
John W. Chadwick.
Caroline J. Chaney.
O. Chanute.
F. J. Child.
L. E. Chittenden.
Joseph H. Choate.
C. T. Christensen.
Percival Chubb.
Frederic E. Church.
Thomas M. Clark.
S. L. Clemens.
Grover Cleveland.
Isaac H. Clothier.
D. H. Cochran.
Charles R. Codman.
Charles Carleton Coffin.
Charles Washington Coleman.
Charles Collins.
Robert Collyer.
Samuel Colman.
Mrs. Samuel Colman.
William J. Coombs.
J. D. Cox.
T. F. Crane.
Frederic Cromwell.
Frederic Crowninshield.
W. E. Cushing.
R. Fulton Cutting.

W. Bayard Cutting.
Chas. P. Daly.
Richard H. Dana.
Ira Davenport.
Richard Harding Davis.
Charles De Garmo.
Margaret Deland.
Horace E. Deming.
Chauncey M. Depew.
Melvil Dewey.
Morgan Dix.
Wm. Croswell Doane.
Mary Mapes Dodge.
Theodore Ayrault Dodge.
W. E. Dodge.
W. H. Draper.
John Drew.
H. Drisler.
D. B. Eaton.
Geo. F. Edmunds.
Edward Eggleston.
Louis R. Ehrich.
Charles W. Eliot.
Richard T. Ely.
Edward W. Emerson.
Wm. Endicott, Jr.
Dana Estes.
Wm. M. Evarts.
Charles S. Fairchild.
Henry W. Farnam.
Loyall Farragut.
Annie Fields.
Charles E. Fitch.
Joseph E. Follett.
Mary Hallock Foote.
J. M. Forbes.
Alcée Fortier.
T. Thomas Fortune.
Wm. D. Foulke.
Austen G. Fox.
David G. Francis.
Daniel Chester French.
O. B. Frothingham.
Henry B. Fuller.
W. H. Furness.

Hamlin Garland.
F. J. Garrison.
Wendell P. Garrison.
Merrill E. Gates.
Charles Gayarré.
W. J. Gaynor.
J. Card. Gibbons.
Wolcott Gibbs.
W. Hamilton Gibson.
R. W. Gilder.
D. C. Gilman.
N. P. Gilman.
Washington Gladden.
Edwin L. Godkin.
Parke Godwin.
Robert Grant.
Edward O. Graves.
R. T. Greener.
Wm. Elliot Griffis.
Edw. E. Hale.
Matthew Hale.
G. Stanley Hall.
Murat Halstead.
J. Henry Harper.
Joseph W. Harper.
William R. Harper.
J. Andrews Harris.
Constance Cary Harrison.
Joseph R. Hawley.
Rowland Hazzard.
Jos. C. Hendrix.
W. T. Hewett.
Abram S. Hewitt.
H. L. Higginson.
James J. Higginson.
Thos. Wentworth Higginson.
A. S. Hill.
Fred. W. Hinrichs.
Ripley Hitchcock.
E. A. Hoffman.
O. W. Holmes.
H. Holt.
Edward W. Hooper.
James K. Hosmer.
Julia Ward Howe.

R. M. Hunt.
D. Huntington.
F. D. Huntington.
Geo. P. Huntington.
W. R. Huntington.
John F. Hurst.
Laurence Hutton.
Wm. DeW. Hyde.
Henry Irving.
D. Willis James.
Henry James.
Thos. L. James.
Wm. James.
Thomas A. Janvier.
Joseph Jastrow.
J. Jefferson.
Morris K. Jesup.
Sarah Orne Jewett.
Eastman Johnson.
Robert Underwood Johnson.
R. M. Johnston.
David Starr Jordan.
John J. Keane.
Charles King.
Coates Kinney.
Gustav E. Kissel.
Thos. W. Knox.
John La Farge.
George Parsons Lathrop.
J. E. Learned.
Walter Learned.
Charlton T. Lewis.
Mary A. Livermore.
H. C. Lodge.
Alice M. Longfellow.
T. R. Lounsbury.
Seth Low.
Wm. G. Low.
Chas. Lyman.
Mary Lyman.
Theodore Lyman.
A. R. Macdonough.
Alexander Mackay-Smith.
Wayne MacVeagh.
W. H. Male.

Jno. Malone.
Henry G. Marquand.
Edward S. Martin.
Edward G. •Mason.
F. O. Mason.
Brander Matthews.
Henry W. Maxwell.
Joseph May.
W. Gordon McCabe.
A. C. McClurg.
C. R. Miller.
F. D. Millet.
W. W. Montgomery.
J. Pierpont Morgan.
Edw'd S. Morse.
John T. Morse, Jr.
Levi P. Morton.
J. Mosenthal.
T. T. Munger.
S. P. Nash.
Henry Loomis Nelson.
Simon Newcomb.
R. Heber Newton.
Virginius Newton.
Wm. Wilberforce Newton.
Charles Nordhoff.
Cyrus Northrop.
Henry A. Oakley.
Geo. M. Olcott.
Fred'k. Law Olmstead.
Oswald Ottendorfer.
Edwin Packard.
Thos. Nelson Page.
Alice Freeman Palmer.
G. H. Palmer.
Charles Parsons.
Jno. E. Parsons.
Robt. E. Pattison.
Francis L. Patton.
Geo. Foster Peabody.
Thomas S. Perry.
Edward L. Pierce.
Henry L. Pierce.
J. Hall Pleasants.
Horace Porter.

Geo. B. Post.
Henry C. Potter.
O. B. Potter.
William Potts.
Edna Dean Proctor.
G. H. Putnam.
W. S. Rainsford.
Julian Ralph.
B. P. Raymond.
E. McKim Reed.
Francis B. Reeves.
Chas. S. Reinhart.
James E. Rhoades.
William T. Richards.
H. A. Richmond.
G. L. Rives.
Sherman S. Rogers.
Theodore Roosevelt.
Wm. E. Russell.
W. G. Russell.
S. N. Ryan.
D. Sage.
H. W. Sage.
F. B. Sanborn.
M. J. Savage.
Wm. C. Schermerhorn.
Chas. A. Schieren.
J. G. Schurman.
C. Schurz.
M. Schuyler.
Austin Scott.
Charles Scribner.
Horace E. Scudder.
L. Clark Seelye.
Frank Sewell.
Helen A. Shafer.
N. S. Shaler.
Edward M. Shepard.
R. R. Sinclair.
W. A. Slater.
Wm. M. Sloane.
G. W. Smalley.
William T. Smedley.
Chas. Emory Smith.
Chas. Stewart Smith.

F. Hopkinson Smith.
Geo. Williamson Smith.
Lizzie W. Smith.
T. Guilford Smith.
Wm. Alex'r Smith.
E. C. Sprague.
Henry H. Sprague.
Edmund C. Stedman.
Francis Lynde Stetson.
Augustus St. Gaudens.
Albert Stickney.
Anson Phelps Stokes.
Moorfield Storey.
Richard S. Storrs.
Russell Sturgis.
Lucius B. Swift.
Mrs. Bayard Taylor.
J. M. Taylor.
John A. Taylor.
Wm. M. Taylor.
Celia Thaxter.
Abbott H. Thayer.
George A. Thayer.
Edith M. Thomas.
Theodore Thomas.
Daniel G. Thompson.
Hugh S. Thompson.
W. H. Thomson.
Charles F. Thwing.
Louis C. Tiffany.
H. A. P. Torrey.
B. F. Tracy.
W. L. Trenholm.
Herbert Tuttle.
Edmund Tweedy.
Kinsley Twining.
Anson Judd Upson.
C. Vanderbilt.
John C. VanDyke.
M. G. Van Rensselaer.
Calvert Vaux.
Elihu Vedder.
Wm. P. Vilas.
Marvin R. Vincent.
D. H. Von Holst.

In pursuance of the charge given it the Committee voted to secure subscriptions for a bronze bust of Mr. Curtis, to be made by John Quincy Adams Ward, and for the establishment of a Fellowship at Columbia University to be known as the "George William Curtis Fellowship."

Such subscriptions having been secured after considerable delay, caused by the financial disturbances of the time, on the second of May, 1899, the Secretary transmitted the Treasurer's check for $10,000 to the Treasurer of Columbia University. Under the terms agreed upon the Fellowship was to be allotted once in three years, and was to be tenable for two years, at a rate presumably of $600 per annum. Since its establishment three appointments have been made, that of Dr. James Wilford Garner in 1900, that of Mr. Charles Austin Beard in 1903, and that of Charles Grove Haines in 1904.

Mr. Ward completed the work entrusted to him three or four years ago, and the Committee voted that the bust should be tendered to the Trustees of the Public Library, to be placed in the new Library Building when that building should be completed. Under date of December 16, 1901, the Trustees accepted the gift.

After considerable delay and partly because of the incomplete state of the Library Building and the length of time before it would be ready for occupancy, it was determined to deposit the bust temporarily in the Lenox Library Building.

In pursuance of this determination, unveiling exercises were had before a small gathering there December 7, 1903. Hon. Seth Low presided and made the presentation, Mr. William Potts unveiled the bust, and Dr. John S. Billings accepted it on behalf of the Trustees of the Library. Hon. Carl Schurz then delivered the following address:

MEMORIAL ADDRESS

BY

HON. CARL SCHURZ.

Among the most inspiring recollections of my life is a scene I witnessed in the Republican National Convention of 1860, which nominated Abraham Lincoln as its candidate for the presidency of the United States. The Convention was about to vote upon the Republican platform reported by the Committee on Resolutions. Then arose the venerable form of Joshua R. Giddings, of Ohio, one of the veteran champions of the anti-slavery cause. He confessed himself painfully surprised that the Declaration of Independence had not found an explicit recognition in that solemn announcement of the Republican creed, and he moved to amend the platform by inserting in a certain place the words: "That the maintenance of the principle promulgated in the Declaration of Independence and embodied in the Federal Constitution that all men are created equal; that they are endowed by their Creator with certain inalienable rights; that among these are life, liberty, and the pursuit of happiness; that to secure those rights governments are instituted among men deriving their just powers from the consent of the governed, is essential to the preservation of our republican institutions." The Convention, impatient, as such assemblages are apt to be, at any proposition threatening to delay the dispatch of business, heedlessly rejected the amendment. Mr. Giddings, a look of distress upon his face, his white head towering above the crowd, slowly and sadly walked toward the door of the hall.

Suddenly from among the New York delegation a young man of strikingly beautiful features leaped upon a chair and demanded to be heard. The same noisy demonstration of

impatience greeted him. But he would not yield. "Gentlemen," he said, in calm tones, "this is a convention of free
speech, and I have been given the floor. I have but a few
words to say to you, but I shall say them if I stand here until
to-morrow morning." Another tumultuous explosion of impatience, but he did not falter. At last his courage won and
silence fell upon the assembly. Then his musical voice rang
out like a trumpet call. Was this, he said, the party of freedom
met on the borders of the free prairies to advance the cause of
liberty and human rights? And would the representatives of
that party dare to reject the doctrine of the Declaration of
Independence affirming the equality and rights of men? After
a few such sentences of almost defiant appeal he renewed the
amendment to the platform moved by Mr. Giddings, and with
an overwhelming shout of enthusiasm the Convention
adopted it.

The young man who did this was George William Curtis.
I had never seen him before. After the adjournment of that
day's session I went to him to thank him for what he had
done. We became friends then and there and remained friends
to the day of his death. He was then in the flower of youthful
manhood. As he stood there in that convention, dauntless
among the seething multitude, his beautiful face radiant with
resolute fervor, his peculiarly melodious voice thrilling with
impassioned anxiety of purpose, one might have seen in him an
ideal, poetic embodiment of the best of that moral impulse and
that lofty enthusiasm which aroused the people of the North
to the decisive struggle against slavery. Nor was the impression he made then weakened by closer acquaintance. All
those who knew him well found him not only to possess in
ample measure the qualities and the lofty inspirations as the
personification of which he had appeared in that memorable
scene, but also that his whole being breathed an exquisite
refinement of moral and æsthetic sense, of ways of thinking,
of manner and speech, which made his friends feel as if he
were almost too gentle a being to be exposed to the ordinary
rude jostlings and buffetings of public life, which those of us
who were made of rougher clay, could well endure.

Nature seemed to have designed him for the republic of letters, and at an early period he gave promise of a literary career of rare distinction. His preparation for that career was indeed not such as the reader of his writings and the listener to his speech would suppose it to have been. He had not passed through the classical course of a college or university, although his personality might have been taken to present the very ideal of a university man. It cannot even be said that he had enjoyed the advantage of a methodical and continuous education of any sort. To be sure he had as a boy had something more than the ordinary elementary schooling. But beyond that he did his reading, and gathered his knowledge, and cultivated his abilities very much according to his own individual tastes and his adventitious opportunities.

His father, a prosperous banker, intended him for commercial pursuits and placed him in a mercantile house. But there he learned quickly that commercial pursuits were not for him.

Seventeen years old he joined for a while, with his brother, Burrill, as a boarder, the famous Brook Farm community, that assemblage of fine moral and intellectual enthusiasms given to the cultivation of somewhat fantastic ideals. There his poetic and, at the same time, soberly discriminating mind accepted all there was of noble inspiration, but kept aloof from extravagant theories. Then, after a winter's round of social pleasures at home in New York, he lived, once more with his brother Burrill, for two years on a farm near Concord, Massachusetts, again studying what he liked,—history, languages, literature, art, philosophy—and, at the same time, enjoying the conversation of Emerson and of the remarkable men that gathered around that sage, and sipping the "transcendentalism" as much as his constantly sober mind could digest and assimilate.

This was all he had in his younger days of what may be called sedentary education. Then his travels begun,—leisurely roamings through Egypt, Syria, Italy, Switzerland, Austria, Germany, France and England—delightful rambles which enriched his imagination, broadened his knowledge of things and men, inspired his artistic instincts, developed the cosmopolitan largeness and justice of his mind, and, giving him much to say and the desire to say it, started him as a productive man of letters. During the four years of travel he described his experiences in the "Courier and Enquirer" and in the "New York Tribune." But after his return in 1851, he published his "Nile Notes of a Howadji" and his "Howadji in Syria," candid, warm-blooded accounts of what he had seen and heard, and felt, the honestly picturesque and innocently glowing realism of which seems to have startled some over-fastidious critics. Then he wrote for "Putnam's Magazine," which had assembled on its staff, with him, such men as the one who in old age became his most brilliant eulogist, Parke Godwin, and Charles F. Briggs, and had among its contributors the most noted American writers of the time. Among his own contributions were that trenchant, although kind-hearted, satire on the follies of the pretentious "society" of those days, the "Potiphar Papers," then the "Homes of American Authors," and that charmingly fantastic well of thought and sentiment, "Prue and I." At last in October, 1853, he sat down in the "Easy Chair" of "Harper's Monthly Magazine," and ten years later he took charge of the editorial page of "Harper's Weekly," from which two positions he continued to speak to the American people to the end of his days.

The exuberance of his fancy, his faculty of keen observation, the wide reach of his knowledge, the geniality of his humor, kindly even in his sarcasm, the exquisite purity and refinement of his diction, the loftiness of his principles, and the nobility and warmth of his enthusiasm gave his writings a charm all their own, and to the reader a full measure of unalloyed delight. But, I am sure, it is not as a literary man alone that we are assembled here to celebrate his memory by unveiling this monument. Eminent, as he was, as a contributor to American letters, he was far more eminent as a public teacher of the highest order—a teacher who taught, by example as well as precept, lessons inspired by the noblest ideals of virtue and patriotism.

I do not mean to say that he confined himself to what might be called literary preaching ; for his deep and ardent public spirit called him in early manhood to the sterner tasks imposed upon him by his conception of civic duty. The anti-slavery cause took hold of his whole moral nature and made him an active member of the Republican party of those days. He was one of the men who advocated anti-slavery principles when it was dangerous to do so, and who exposed themselves not only to partisan reviling in speech and press but to physical violence in facing infuriated mobs. It was the moral courage of his convictions which kept him calm and resolute on a platform in Philadelphia when clubs and brickbats appeared to answer the anti-slavery argument.

But his political career was, in some respects, essentially different from that of most men of ability and ambition who devote themselves to the service of the public. While he unceasingly labored with pen and speech for what he thought right, and just, and honorable, not selecting for himself, like a fastidious dilettante only the dainty part of the work, but plunging personally into the rough encounter with the partisan opponent as well as, on his own side, with the professional politician in primary, caucus and convention, he declined for himself those rewards which even a perfectly legitimate personal ambition might have coveted. Although a man of his brilliant abilities, splendid working force and charming personality, might easily have risen to high places of distinction and power, he sought for himself nothing but the station and the opportunities of the simple public spirited citizen, looking for his own recompense only to the good he might accomplish for his country and mankind. He declined the high honor of the mission to England, a post in which his exceptionally fine qualities would have shown to the utmost advantage, but he accepted the comparatively humble chairmanship of the Civil Service Commission, because there he hoped to do a work which strongly appealed to his sense of patriotic duty.

After the abolition of slavery the reform of the civil service was the cause dearest to his heart. In the brutal barbarism of the spoils system and the far-reaching demoralization of our political life springing from it, he saw not only a grave danger to our free institutions, but also a dishonor to the American name. This scandalous abuse not only alarmed him as a statesman, but it also wounded his pride as an American citizen.

He threw the whole enthusiasm and energy of his nature into the struggle against it. At the head of a small body of men of the same faith he led in the struggle. He had to combat the greed of the professional politicians who drew from the patronage their means of livelihood, and the hostility of more aspiring public men who found a well drilled organization of mercenary henchmen necessary for their maintenance in power. He had to overcome also the lethargy of the public mind, which inertly adhered to long established custom. It seemed to be an almost hopeless contest, and disappointment followed disappointment.

But he joined to the enthusiasm of the idealist the tough tenacity of purpose which is inspired by true conviction. After every failure he patiently resumed the Sisyphean task of heaving the stone uphill, until at last it found a lodgment. Congress as well as some State Legislatures enacted laws rescuing a large part of the public service from the curse of spoils politics. But this was only a beginning; and with unflagging watchfulness and zeal he endeavored to fortify the positions won and to push on the advance.

Without injustice to others whose part in the work can not be overlooked, it may well be said that Curtis, by his wide knowledge and experience, his ripe and calm judgment, his gentle temper, and his scarcely asserted but easily acknowledged authority, was most perfectly fitted for that essential task of leadership in such a cause—the task of reconciling the diversities of opinion, and of harmonizing, stimulating and directing the zeal and the efforts of others laboring for the same object. He was not only the President of the National Civil Service Reform League, re-elected from year to year, without any question, as a matter of course, but he was also to the day of his death, more than any other person, the intellectual head, the guiding force and the constant moral inspiration of the civil service reform movement. The addresses he delivered at the annual meetings of the league were like mile-stones in the progress of the work, and, as he reported to the country what had been done and what was still to be done, and why and wherefore, enlightening the public mind and cheering on his fellow laborers, the spoils politicians had to listen with respect and wonder—unwilling perhaps—to the voice of a devotion, the perfeet unselfishness of which nobody could doubt, and of a quiet energy which no obstacle and no failure could dismay, and which, slowly but steadily, drove them from one entrenchment to another.

The civil service reform movement acting upon the public mind, without resort to any of the contrivances of party machinery, by a perfectly intellectual and moral influence, and by compelling by such means the spoils politician to surrender from his stubborn grasp one after another of his fields of prey, is one of the most remarkable and cheering proofs of the power of an enlightened public opinion in our time. And of that intellectual and moral influence George William Curtis was the fairest exponent and representative. While the successes won are still incomplete and not uncontested, yet the eyes of the leader closed upon a vastly improved public sentiment and upon results which cannot be undone; and when, at some future day, the reform of the civil service in the widest sense is an accomplished fact, as it surely will be, the American people, while justly recognizing the merits of others, will gratefully remember George William Curtis as one of the bravest pioneers and champions, and as the true hero of that great achievement.

He was a warm and faithful party man so long as the objects pursued by his party were such as not to offend his conscience. He broke with his party when he became convinced that its conduct made it an instrument of evil to the country. It was not upon a mere quick impulse, or with a light heart that he took the decisive step. The party which had fought the great battle against slavery was very dear to him. In it he had formed associations to which he was most warmly attached and which it gave him the keenest pangs of pain to sever. Only the stern voice of duty could move him to give up all this. How much he sacrificed, and how much more he risked, when in 1884 he declared himself against a Republican candidate for the Presidency, only those know who stood nearest to him.

No conspicuous member of a party can turn away from it without exposing himself to bitter censure and vituperation. This was also his lot. It seems to be extremely difficult to the ordinary partisan mind to understand how a man of conscience may abandon his party allegiance in order to maintain his allegiance to his principles and his convictions of right. To the common run of party politicians fidelity to the organization is the highest of political virtues, even when it involves faithless ness to a great cause, and he denounces severance from the organization as a sort of felony, even when it is demanded by fidelity to the faith always professed. No doubt Curtis felt keenly the obloquy that was poured upon him. But he had at least the high satisfaction of receiving from his very opponents a rare tribute to the nobility of his character. Even the most wanton ebullitions of an exasperated party spirit hardly ever went so far as seriously to impugn the purity of his motives.

He was the finest type of the independent in politics. While fully recognizing the usefulness and even the necessity of political parties in a government like ours, he never forgot that a party is after all only a means to an end, and not an end itself. He considered and discussed questions of public interest on their own merits—for this is the true essence of conscientious independence. He carefully weighed in his judgment the question, the success of which party or candidate would be most beneficial to the public good, and then awarded his support or opposition according to the conviction so formed, unawed by power or popular clamor, and unbiased by favor or personal friendship—and in all this there was no man more dutifully respecting the constituted authorities, or more kindly heeding the opinions of others, or more loyal as a friend to his friends.

But however strenuous his political activity in the public arena may have been from time to time, it did not interrupt his editorial work. He steadily continued his tranquil and genial talks in the "Easy Chair" of Harper's Magazine—talks which were in good part called forth by passing occurrences, and roamed over almost every field of human interest. And even now when the happenings or conditions which occasioned them, have long been forgotten, or live only in dim reminiscence, the "Easy Chair" papers can still be read with delightful enjoyment as entertaining literature, full as they are of animated pictures of life, of instructive suggestions, or keen judgments, and, without obtrusive moralizing, of elevating sentiment.

And as the political editor and leading writer of the widely circulating Harper's Weekly, he unceasingly spoke to the untold thousands of his countrymen all over the land; and all those thousands felt that every word he said to them was the truth as understood by an honest intellect and a great heart; that he always endeavored to discover the truth by conscientious inquiry and careful consideration; that every praise he bestowed and every censure he pronounced on any public man or any political party, was dictated by the most scrupulous desire to be just; that his very denunciations were tempered with charity; and that every advice he gave was prompted by the most unselfish zeal for the honor and true greatness of the republic and the elevation and happiness of the people. They had, even when their opinions differed from his, instinctive confidence in the purity of the source from which the utterances flowed; they knew that in that source there was nothing of greed, nothing of envy, nothing of vain pride of opinion—nothing but an ardent love of his country, and of liberty and justice, and a profound devotion to the highest ideals of human civilization.

But however effective his regular journalistic communion with the public was, the most valuable and impressive of his teachings were contained in that grand series of orations and occasional addresses which not only placed him in the first rank of the great orators of his time, but also constitute his finest contributions to American literature—addresses and orations delivered at college commencements, alumni reunions, the unveiling of monuments, memorial services in honor of statesmen, or soldiers, or men of letters, or public meetings held to shape, or express, or stimulate popular sentiment on some matter of great public concern. Nothing could surpass the splendid architecture of their argument and the wealth and chaste beauty of their ornamentation. In what gorgeous colors he would paint the glories of his country! How he would revel in the memories of the heroic birth of the republic and in extolling the grand and eternal significance of the principles which constituted its reason of being and its promise to all mankind! With what lofty sternness he would castigate those whose mean spirit failed to appreciate those principles! How vividly he would make to gleam and radiate the virtues and high aims and achievements of the great men who were the subjects of his eulogy! How magnificently his noble manhood and his American citizen pride shone forth when he defined to the youth of his generation the nature of true patriotism—a patriotism that embraced all the human kind and had its source in the purest moral sense and in the profoundest and most courageous convictions of right and duty in the service of the highest ideals!

We shall know the character and the principles of the man best when we let him speak for himself in his own language. Listen to these words he uttered to the Phi Beta Kappa Society of Harvard, addressing them on "The American Doctrine of Liberty": "The real patriot in this country is *he* who sees most clearly what the nation *ought* to desire, who does what he can by plain and brave speech to influence it to that desire, and then urges and supports the laws which express it. But as public opinion is necessarily so powerful with us, we fear and flatter it, and so pamper it into a tyrant. How the country teems with conspicuous men, scholars, orators, politicians, divines, advocates,—public teachers all, whose speeches, sermons, letters, votes, actions, are a prolonged, incessant falsehood and sophism; a soft and shallow wooing of the Public Alexander and the Public Cromwell, telling him that he has no crook in his neck and no wart on his nose! How many of our public men and famous orators have said not what they thought, rather what they supposed we wanted to hear? In a system like ours where almost every man has a vote, and votes as he chooses, public opinion is really the government. Whoever panders to it, is training a tyrant for our master. Whoever enlightens it lifts the people toward peace and prosperity." To teach the people what they *ought* to desire, that is the office of patriotic leadership.

He pursued this subject with the intensest earnestness.

"Patriotism," he said to the graduating class of Union College, "patriotism is like the family instinct. In the child it is a blind devotion; in the man an intelligent love. The patriot perceives the claim made upon his country by the circumstances and time of her growth and power, and how God is to be served by using those opportunities of helping mankind. Therefore his country's honor is dear to him as his own, and he would as soon lie and steal himself as assist or excuse his country in a crime. Right and wrong, justice and crime, exist independently of our country. A public wrong is not a private right for any citizen. The citizen is a man bound to know and do the right, and the nation is but an aggregation of citizens. If a man shouts: "My country, by whatever means extended and bounded, my country right or wrong," he merely utters words such as those might be of the thief who steals in the street, or of the trader who swears falsely at the Custom-House, both of them chuckling: "My fortune, however acquired!"

"Remember," said he on another occasion, "remember that the greatness of our country is not in the greatness of its (material) achievements, but in its promise—a promise that cannot be fulfilled without that sovereign moral sense, without a sensitive moral conscience.—Commercial prosperity is only a curse if it be not subservient to moral and intellectual progress, and our prosperity will conquer us if we do not conquer our prosperity. Our commercial success tends to make us all cowards; but we have got to make up our minds in this country whether we believe in the power and goodness of God as sincerely as we undoubtedly do in the dexterity of the devil; that we may shape our national life accordingly, and not be praying now to good God, and now to good devil, and wondering which is going to carry us off after all. The whole of patriotism seems to consist at the present moment in the maintenance of this public moral tone. No voice of self-glorification, no complacent congratulation that we are the greatest, wisest, and best of nations will help our greatness and goodness in the smallest degree. Are we satisfied that America should have no other excuse for independent national existence than a superior facility of money-making? Why, if we are unfaithful as a nation, though our population were to double in a year, and the roar and rush of our vast machinery were to silence the music of the spheres, and our wealth were enough to buy all the world, our population could not bully history, nor all our riches bribe the eternal justice not to write upon us 'Ichabod, Ichabod, thy glory is departed!' But I am not here to counsel you to despair and head shakings. I am here to-day that this country which you are to inherit, and for which you are to be responsible, needs only an enlightened patriotism to fulfil all its mission and justify the dreams of its youth."

Equally high was his conception of government. "The object of government," he said in an address on the duty of the American scholar, "the object of government is human liberty. Laws restrain the encroachment of the individual upon society in order that all individuals may be secured the freest play of their powers. This is because the end of society is the improvement of the individual and the development of the race. Liberty is, therefore, the condition of human progress, and consequently that is the best government which gives to men the largest liberty, and constantly modifies itself in the interest of freedom."

And further in his oration on patriotism: "Our government was established confessedly in obedience to this sentiment of human liberty. And your duty as patriots is to understand clearly that by all its antecedents your country is consecrated to the cause of freedom; that it was discovered when the great principle of human liberty was about to be organized in institutions; that it was settled by men who were exiled by reason of their loyalty to that principle; that it separated from its mother-country because that principle had been assailed; that it began its peculiar existence by formally declaring its faith in human freedom and equality; and, therefore, that whatever in its government policy tends to destroy that freedom and equality is Anti-American and unpatriotic, because America and Liberty are inseparable ideas."

Listen to his thoughts upon the relation of the citizen to his party—and he said this when he was still a party-man of regular standing: "The most plausible suspicion of the permanence of the American government is founded in the belief that party spirit cannot be restrained. The first object of concerted political action is the highest welfare of the country. But the conditions of party association are such that the means are constantly and easily substituted for the end. The sophistry is subtle and seductive. Holding the ascendancy of his party essential to the national welfare, the zealous partisan merges patriotism in party. He insists that not to sustain the party is to betray the country; and against all honest doubt and reasonable hesiation and reluctance he vehemently urges that quibbles of conscience must be sacrificed to the public good; that wise and practical men will not be squeamish; that every soldier in the army cannot indulge his whims; and that if the majority may justly prevail in determining the government, it must not be questioned in the control of a party. His spirit adds moral coercion to sophistry. It denounces as a traitor him who protests against party tyranny, and it makes unflinching adherence to what is called regular party action, the condition of the gratification of honorable political ambition. Because a man, who sympathizes with the party aims, refuses to vote for a thief, this spirit scorns him as a rat and a renegade. Because he holds to principle and law against party expediency and dictation, he is proclaimed as the betrayer of his country, justice and humanity. Because he tranquilly insists upon deciding for himself when he must dissent from his party, he is reviled as a popinjay and visionary fool. Seeking with honest purpose only the welfare of his country, the hot air around him hums with the cry of 'the grand old party,' 'the traditions of the party,' 'loyalty to the party,' 'future of the party,' 'servants of the party,' and he sees and hears the gorged and portly money changers in the temple usurping the very divinity of the God. Young hearts, be not dismayed! If even any one of you shall be the man so denounced, do not forget that your own individual convictions are the whips of small cords which God has put into your hands to expel the blasphemers. Perfect party discipline is the most dangerous weapon of party spirit, for it is the abdication of individual judgment; it is the application to political parties of the Jesuit principle of implicit obedience. It is for you (the academic youth) to help break this withering spell. When you are angrily told that, if you erect your individual judgment against the regular party behest, you make representative government impossible by refusing to accept its conditions, hold fast by your conscience and let the party go. The remedy for the constant excess of party spirit lies, and lies alone, in the courageous independence of the individual citizen."

And with what words of fire he addressed the representatives of the press, he himself being a working journalist: "I need not be told that an editor may be an honest partisan. We all probably belong to a party not alone in great emergencies of the State, but upon general principles and tendencies of government we must all take sides. Naturally the army in whose ranks we march becomes identified with the cause. Its colors, its music, its battlecries become those of the cause itself. So a man comes to confound his party with his country, and to be wholly partisan seems to him to be only patriotic. Associated with illustrious achievements for his country and for man-kind, the party name becomes as sweet to his ear and heart as, after famous victories, the name of his regiment to a soldier. But this is only the romantic and poetic aspect of one of the greatest perils of popular government. We liken a party to an army, and the phrases of an election are military terms. But an army is not a cause; it is merely an agency. A party is not a principle and an end; it is only a means. It is the abject servility which is bred by the military spirit that has made a standing army the standing threat of liberty. As the servility of the military spirit is a standing peril of liberty, so the servility of party spirit is the standing peril of popular government. This servility to party spirit is the abdication of that moral leadership of opinion which is the great function of the political press. It is a subserviency which destroys the independence of the paper, but it does not save the party. There is not a party in the history of this country which has been utterly overthrown, that might not have survived long and victoriously, if its press had been courageously independent. The press submits to be led by party leaders, while its duty is to lead leaders. They dare to disgrace their party, to expose it to humiliation and defeat, because they count upon the slavery of the party press. The press is never a more beneficent power than when it disappoints this malignant expectation and shows the country that, while loyal to a party and its policy, it is more loyal to honor and patriotism. This is the independence of the press. It is not non-partisanship nor impotent neutrality. It is not the free lance of an Italian bravo or soldier of fortune at the disposal of the master who pays the best. It is not the unprincipled indifference which cries to-day 'good Lord' and to-morrow 'good devil' as the Lord or the devil seems to be prevailing. Nor is it a daily guess how the wind is going to blow, and a dexterous conformity to what it believes to be public opinion. No paper and no man who fears to be in the minority has the power to create a majority. It is the unquailing advocacy of its own principles when it stands alone, and honorable support of a party when a party proclaims them; it is scorn of falsehood and baseness and bribery in sustaining them; it is manly justice to opponents and unsparing exposure of offenders and offenses which, disgracing the party, tend to weaken and destroy it; it is austere allegiance to high ideals of public virtue and perfect reliance upon the ultimate justice of the people—it is all this which makes an independent press the greatest power in Christendom."

As he taught the sanctity of conscience as against party, so he taught the sanctity of conscience as against the majority. "In a republic," he said in an address on the leadership of educated men, "as the majority must control action, the majority constantly tends to usurp control of opinion. Its decree is accepted as the standard of right and wrong. To differ is grotesque and eccentric. To protest is preposterous. To defy is incendiary and revolutionary. But just here interposes educated intelligence and asserts the worth of self reliance and the power of the individual conscience. Gathering the wisdom of ages as into a sheaf of sunbeams it shows that progress springs from the minority, and that if it will but stand fast, time will give it the victory. And further it is educated citizenship which, while defining the rightful limitation of the power of the majority, is most loyal to its legitimate authority, and foremost always in rescuing it from the treachery of political peddlers and parasites."

The highest praise he bestowed on James Russell Lowell in his magnificent eulogy was in these words, which he might have spoken of himself: "Literature was his pursuit, but patriotism was his passion. His love of country was that of a lover for his mistress. He resented the least imputation upon his ideal America, and nothing was finer than his instinctive scorn for the pinchbeck patriotism which brags and boasts and swaggers, insisting that bigness is greatness, and vulgarity, simplicity, and the will of the majority the moral law."

With a boldness which may startle many of those who swim in the political currents of to-day, he defined his conception of the Republican soldier in a memorial address on General Sedgwick delivered in October, 1868, at West Point, the seat of our great military academy. "In your name and in your presence," said he, "here in the school in which our officers are trained, I deny that to become a soldier is to cease to be a citizen and a man. I deny that a soldier is a moral monster for whom right and wrong do not exist. I deny that in a noble breast, whether in or out of uniform, the sense of loyalty to the flag will be dearer and stronger than that of loyalty to conscience and to manhood. And if our own heaven-born Stars and Stripes should ever become the black flag of infamy and injustice, it is an insult to you, as to your fellow citizens to suppose that you or they would imagine it to be an honorable duty to bear it. We are citizens of the world before we are citizens of any country; we are men before we are Americans—*ubi libertas, ibi patria*—and our duty as Americans is to make America the home of noble men, and that flag the flag of liberty for mankind."

As portrayed by his own utterances this was George William Curtis as a public character and a public teacher—the ideal party man; for he always strove to the utmost to hold his party true to its highest aims; and the ideal independent, being true to his principles, his convictions of right and the commands of his conscience even against the behests of his party. And as he was the ideal party man and the ideal independent, so he might well have been called the finest type of the American gentleman.

He was intensely proud of his country without ever being boastful. He would have stood in the company of kings without embarassment, but also without making any demonstrative display of his feeling himself at ease. He was not ashamed of not being rich. Indeed, he took good care not to *become* rich, by voluntary assuming and laboriously working to pay off obligations of friends and associates, to which he could never have been legally held, and for which only a most susceptible sense of honor could detect any sort of responsibility on his part. He possessed that true politeness which consists in an instinctive regard for the feelings of others and springs from genuine kindness of heart. His exquisite refinement of taste and manner had not the slightest tinge of affectation or superciliousness. No coarse utterance ever crossed his lips because no coarse thought or sentiment ever crossed his soul. He made his inferiors feel at home in his presence by gladly recognizing their merits without the faintest air of condescending superiority. He was a distinguished man in the most distinguished society, moving in it with unpretending naturalness, and appearing only what he really was. When we think of the men whom we would point out as models to our youth at home, or whom we would like to have looked upon as representative American gentlemen by the world abroad, George William Curtis will surely be selected as one of the first.

What his pure, gentle, lovable and loving nature was to those standing nearest to him, no words can express. If his personal friends speak of him only in the language of eulogy, it is because it will sound like eulogy when they speak of him only the sober truth as they understand and feel it. He was indeed one of those rare human beings in whom the eye of criticism detects nothing that friendship would care to conceal; and it may well be said that nobody ever came into contact with him without being better and happier for it.

It is a saddening thought that the melody of his eloquent voice will never be heard again, and that his ennobling presence is gone from among us forever. We have to console ourselves with the certainty that much of his work will endure, that the inspiration of his teaching and example will live, and that his memory will be tenderly cherished and remain highly honored as that of a benefactor of mankind and one of the noblest citizens of our republic.

CPSIA information can be obtained
at www.ICGtesting.com
Printed in the USA
BVHW04*1206070818
523813BV00007B/52/P

9 780484 902182